A
Different
Definition

W.T. SWOFFORD

WestBow·
PRESS
A DIVISION OF THOMAS NELSON
& ZONDERVAN

A Different Definition. Title seems pretty catchy and interesting, but I cannot say it came from any thoughts of my own. Also I cannot say the words in this book are all from my own mind. Jesus spoke of a much better definition and it has been recorded in Matthew 5, 6, and 7. In my personal opinion I would much rather you read that collection over mine. But, if you do continue to read I pray that this book is merely a reflection of the "Different Definition" of life Jesus spoke so much about. If any of my pride comes through I apologize. All these things I first write to myself. Let God be in your reading and let Him show you the gift of life He freely gives.

Scripture taken from the New King James Version. Copyright 1979, 1980, 1982 by Thomas Nelson, inc. Used by permission. All rights reserved.

WestBow Press books may be ordered through booksellers or by contacting:

WestBow Press
A Division of Thomas Nelson & Zondervan
1663 Liberty Drive
Bloomington, IN 47403
www.westbowpress.com
1 (866) 928-1240

ISBN: 978-1-4908-3749-9 (sc)
ISBN: 978-1-4908-3748-2 (e)

Library of Congress Control Number: 2014909022

Printed in the United States of America.

WestBow Press rev. date: 05/30/2014

1

SIN

Even as a small child we had our own definition of sin. To sin was to do something bad, to lie, cheat, steal; or if we were a BIG sinner to murder. We knew to sin was wrong, and if we sinned we were to be punished. Our lifestyle was defined by this definition of sin. If we weren't sinning we believed everything would go good in life, but if we were having troubles it meant we were sinning. Many live their whole life with these thoughts and in all reality, it seems like a decent way to go through life. But how is sin really defined?

One of the earliest accounts of sin was in the Roman army. The Roman archers used levels of sin to define how much they missed their target by. If they missed the bulls eye, or the center of the target, that was a sin. Their main goal in practice or combat was to "not sin" and hit what they were aiming for. This would seem like a good way to demonstrate how we as followers of Christ sin, but most of the time this couldn't be any further from it. Not only

1

are we missing the mark, most of the time we aren't even shooting at the right target! We get so caught up in ourselves and this world that often we forget what we are aiming for. And without shooting at the right target, how will we know just how far off the mark we really are?

When you look up the word *sin* in today's dictionary we find something similar to this:

SIN-noun

a: *an offense against religious or moral law*

b : an action that is or is felt to be highly reprehensible <it's a sin to waste food>

This definition goes right in line with what we already seem to believe. An action that is felt to be highly reprehensible; or in simpler words, something that makes us feel BAD. But what about sin makes us feel bad? Do we feel bad because we did something bad? Or do we feel bad because we were being disobedient to someone who told us not to? If we look back close to 180 years ago, we will find that the definition of sin was much different than in the dictionaries today. In the first *American Dictionary of the English Language*, written by Noah Webster in 1828, the definition for sin was as follows:

SIN, n.

1. The voluntary departure of a moral agent from a known rule of rectitude or duty, prescribed by God; any voluntary transgression of the divine law, or violation of a divine command; a wicked act; iniquity. Sin is either a positive act in which a known divine law is violated, or it is the voluntary neglect

to obey a positive divine command, or a rule of duty clearly implied in such command. Sin comprehends not action only, but neglect of known duty, all evil thoughts purposes, words and desires, whatever is contrary to God's commands or law.

Sin isn't just something that makes you feel bad, although that is a general side effect of it. Sin is what occurs when you voluntarily disobey God! The definition by Noah Webster states it clearly; "Sin comprehends not only action, but neglect of known duty". We know right from wrong. We know our duty. It is clearly stated. God has given us a way to live by, and He wants us to live this way so we can draw into a relationship with Him. It is for our own good. The problem is that we think we can find our own way of life and we turn away from God's guidance. When we start to live life on our own is when things really start to get messed up.

The thing is God can have nothing to do with sin. God has never sinned and never will sin. It's not because He can't. God can do anything. But because He is so much more righteous and holy than we can even fathom. Our sin distances us from Him. If this were all there was to say about sin it would be a tragedy. Thankfully, God also believes in these things called grace and mercy. (which I still don't truly understand) God cared enough about us to send His Son Jesus Christ to live a perfect and holy life without sin, and then to die on the cross as punishment for our sins. Before this a sacrifice had to take place of our sins. But for us, Jesus became the ultimate sacrifice! He did nothing wrong. He never sinned. Yet He died to save us. This was the only way that our sins could ultimately be forgiven. Jesus came to free us from our sins. Our lives our now *perfect* through Jesus Christ!

I'll admit this is still hard for me to even believe sometimes. We are free. But not only are we free, we are perfect.

"For He made Him who knew no sin to be sin for us, that we might become the righteousness of God in Him" 2 Corinthians 5:21

Jesus Christ took our sins; present, past, future. He became us and in exchange we get to be Him in the face of God. What that means is that if we are believers in Christ when God looks at us He doesn't see your sin and your failures. He sees a perfect and righteous you.

God has overcome sin for us! We know this to be true. But if we truly believe this, then why are we still living like Jesus never died for us? Jesus came so that we may LIVE, but if you looked at our lives you would think we had nothing to live for. Why is this? Why can't we get passed our sin? I don't believe it's because we don't believe. I believe it's because we see sin as something different from what it actually is.

Sin Is a Choice

Sin is a choice. Whether we want to believe it or not, we choose to disobey God. Sin doesn't just take over us and make the wrong decision for us. When we sin we voluntarily make that decision. If we are to ever get and understanding on what "sin" is we must first realize this. God didn't make us sin. Did God know we were going to sin when He created us? I believe He did. But did He give us the choice not to? *Absolutely*! He gave Adam and Eve full reign in the garden, the only thing they couldn't do was eat of one tree. And believe it or not, this one rule was too much. They couldn't do it, they just had to eat of it. (unfortunately, just like I would have) Now many might say, "But they were tricked and tempted by the Devil." Yes they were, but ultimately it was still their choice to physically eat the fruit. This is our biggest mistake, too many times we blame the Devil for making us sin. Yes the Devil is real, and he has come to seek, kill, and destroy, and don't you ever forget that! But we also too easily forget that the Devil is defeated and has no power over us if we are in Christ! The Devil might tempt us and steer us in the wrong direction, but if we think he makes us sin we're giving him way too much credit. When we sin we do it all on our own. We don't need any help. Sin comes down to seeing two choices, the right and the wrong one, then choosing the wrong one. It is that simple. And it is just as easy to make the right one, but more times than not we choose wrong one.

The right choice is a choice we can make if we choose to. It is possible. I know this for a fact because Jesus Christ did it! He was tempted and tried by life and by the Devil just like we are without falter. Now are we Jesus? Absolutely not! But did He show us that a sinless life is possible? *Yes.* Is it possible for anyone on this earth to live a sinless life besides Jesus? The answer to that is no, we humans are flawed. We are too proud of ourselves to ever be that righteous on our own. But what is keeping us from trying? It is the pursuit that draws us closer, and without falling we could never grow. This is what we must realize. Even though it is our own choice, and we will inevitably fall, it is not a losing battle. God has already won the war for us! So what have we got to lose in giving it our best and trying as hard as we can to make the right choice when presented with the wrong one?

The Pursuit

"It is the pursuit that draws us closer, and without falling we could never grow." This quote, although I don't know where I got it from, is almost a perfect way to describe life. Previously the the question was asked: "So what have we got to lose in giving it our best and trying as hard as we can to make the right choice when presented with the wrong one?" Even though it seems redundant, I'll ask it again. What have we got to lose? The answer is nothing! We were nothing to begin with until God created us, so the least we could do is to live our lives in a pursuit to glorify Him as much as possible.

Yes we are going to fall, but falling is a must if we ever want to grow in a relationship with God. We ourselves are to prideful. We think we can do it on our own, but we absolutely cannot. The only way we can live this life abundantly is if we trust completely in the Lord. To get us to this point of faith God has to first break us down. A lot of times He does this through our sin. At the moment in life when we think we are higher than any other, God will give us a choice and we will make the wrong one. We sin and then we "feel bad" and that is how we are broken. No one thinks that they can be broken, but God will prove them otherwise. Everyone is weak without God. That is why when we are not constantly talking to God we begin to fall. But each and every time we fall, God picks us up again; and every time He breaks us he builds us stronger. This is how we grow in Him. Without sin there would be no way to humble us to the point where all we are seeking is God and a relationship with Him.

"And Jesus said, For judgment I have come into this world, that those who do not see me may see, and that those who see may be made blind." John 9:39

For us to be in a relationship with God we must first humble ourselves. We are nowhere near who He is! So why do we keep trying to be above Him? That's what we do when we sin. "We are saying I don't like the way you told me to live, I'm going to live my own way." God sent Jesus for a purpose! Jesus above all died for our sins, and never forget that! But He also came to show us how to live. He lived a perfect life. He was tempted, tried, and broken down just like me and you, but He did not give in. Although we can never be Jesus, and we will all fall many, many, many times, Jesus showed us that we can overcome ourselves. And that pursuit of trying to become more and more like Jesus is not a losing battle, it is what brings us closer.

Sin is Separation

"What shall we say then? Shall we continue in sin that grace may abound? Certainly not! How shall we who died to sin live any longer in it?" Romans 6:1-2

We give sin too much power. Yes, sin is evil, but how much power does it actually have on us? I believe we give too much credit to sin. It is US! God has given us more than you can even imagine. Have you realized He conquered sin through His Son Jesus Christ?! Once we believe, and die to Christ we ARE no longer enslaved by sin!

"For he who has died has been freed from sin!" Romans 6:7

Jesus took the guilt and shame and awfulness of our sin when He died on the cross. He did this so we could be one with Christ and not have to feel those things. He did this so we could LIVE! Why then do we still feel like our sin keeps us from God?

God hates sin. Yes, we understand that. And if we are in sin God cannot be around it, true also. But what would be false to think is that after Jesus Christ died for our sins that we have to live life scared of sin! Yes, sin hurts God, but we are forgiven. Even further, we are forgiven of sins we have yet to commit. This I still have yet to truly understand. What I do know is that we no longer have to feel the guilt and shame after sin. We can still be one with God. I believe the true separation from God comes from ourselves. When we sin we can't forgive ourselves for what we have done. We feel guilty that we disobeyed God, and we don't believe we are good enough to be saved by God's Grace. And truthfully, we aren't. But guess what; God did it anyway! So stop feeling sorry for yourself and keeping yourself from God, because God has His arms open wide for you to come back to Him. God hates the separation between you and Him just as much as you do. God wants to know you and be with you every step of your life. Stop hindering yourself from honoring Him. When you sin, remember it, but also forget it! Remember what you did wrong so that you can continue your pursuit, but forget it at the same time and know that Jesus Christ wiped your slate clean. To God we are perfect through Jesus Christ. This is something we might not be able to truly understand, but it is an ABSOLUTE TRUTH! God doesn't want to live your life in shame and guilt; He wants you to live in unity with Him!

"What fruit did you have then in the things of which you are now ashamed? For the end of those things is death." Romans 6:21

Change

Even though sin is our choice, change is something we can't do on our own. God is the only one who can change who He made. The thing is we must make the choice to be willing to let God change us. We can't be slaves to both sin and to God. You are the slave of which one you "obey." In order to become a slave to God we must empty ourselves daily. This can only be done when you let go of yourself and who you have become and let God make you someone new. When you let God take over He will change your heart and your mind. You will have different thoughts, different ideas, and different dreams. You will look at your life differently. He changes you. And believe me; He has great things in store for you, all you have to do is make the choice.

So what am I trying to say through all this? If you don't get anything else get this. Sin is bad, but God is much, much greater. We don't have to feel ashamed for our sin any longer. God has freed us from sin. So please, make the choice to pursue Christ every day. And when you do fall, don't separate yourself from God, because you are forgiven. You are no longer "slaves to sin" but are now "slaves to righteousness."

"But now having been set free from sin, and having become slaves of God, you have your fruit to holiness, and the end, everlasting life!"
Romans 6:22

2
NEW LOVE

"I Love you"

Three simple words used every day in many different languages. Although simple, these words can mean so much. They express to someone how you feel and care about them. They are a symbol for a passion; a relationship. Love is a crazy thing. We can spend our entire lives trying to understand it and get nowhere. Love isn't something you can fully comprehend in one lifetime, but finding these glimpses of love is what life is all about.

What Does it Really Mean?

Love. What does it really mean? We all have our own definitions. Many think love is earned. Others think it's achieved, or maybe they think love just takes time. Does it really? Love takes time? Why? Why can't we love immediately? I see a person walking down the street, first time I've ever seen them, but yet I love them. Without them saying a word to me I love them. The way I show this love towards them makes all the difference, and the way you show love tells someone how you define it. Love can be shown or demonstrated in many ways and is defined in even more.

Love [luhv] noun

- *Any object of warm affection or devotion*
- *A strong positive emotion of regard and affection*
- *Have a great affection or liking for*
- *Get pleasure from*

All these definitions try to describe love, and many do a good job. Love is definitely strong and emotional. Love is of course affectionate and devotion is key. You obviously have to like someone to love them; most of the time. And yes, there is a great pleasure in loving someone. But, are these the main goals of love? Is that all there is? It's not until we really start to realize what love is that we begin to see these definitions don't fully define it. Gaining pleasure from love is a side effect, yes; but not the main goal. A strong positive emotion isn't always regarded as affectionate, often times it's lust. And if you told me that you always like the person you love, I'd have to call you a liar. Love goes beyond these things, into a realm we hardly know anything about.

Love goes deeper than just the outward feelings. Outward feelings can deceive us, and make us see something that isn't there. Finding love takes the effort of going digging deeper than the surface. Love is seeing someone for who they are; good and bad, accepting their faults, and not thinking any different of them. Love is not knowing anything about someone and be willing to be their friend for life; no matter what.

In the games of tennis and squash love is a score of zero. A score of 30-0 in a tennis match would be declared to the audience as "Love thirty." This may seem all of irrelevant to you, but when it comes to love tennis and squash have it absolutely right. Love is giving yourself a score of zero, and putting others way before yourself. Love is caring so much that you would be willing to die for someone just so they wouldn't have to feel an ounce of pain.

Love is not earned or achieved! If it was it wouldn't be love, because how could we as humans ever earn or achieve the love of God? He made us....out of nothing! He gave us the breath of life! I have no clue what that means, but I know I don't deserve it! His love is unfathomable. He knew all of my faults, all my failures. He knew every time I would let Him down. He knew this all before He even created the world, but yet He still made me! His love is ridiculous! I can only wish to show a glimpse of His love. For I am so far away from what love really is that I don't even feel like I should call it the same thing. God's love is a new love we have not even begun to figure out.

A "New" Love

What if we started talking about a "New Love"? A different definition of the word. New Love wouldn't be love as you know it. This kind of love doesn't judge, is never jealous, and has no agenda. This New Love wouldn't have to be earned, but was always received. With New Love we would just love! Unfortunately, we hardly ever see this love.

Instead of having a "love all" mentality, we love in degrees. We have our love for our family, our friends, girlfriend, boyfriend, wife, husband, etc. Each has their place in our heart, but each one we would be willing to do more or less for. We want to say we love everyone, but do we really? Put away what this world tells us about love and focus on what it really means. Love is truly seeing no difference in each man or woman. Love is seeing everyone as equals, no matter what they have done. Can we truly love enough to see everyone the same?

Look at the person walking down the street. This person you don't know, have never talked to them in your life, and might not get along with. Could you love them with everything you have? Would you be willing to give up your life for theirs? Could you physically die so that a total stranger would be saved from just one painful moment? For this is what New Love ultimately is. Love is shown in many different ways, but New Love is shown through sacrifice. New Love comes through when you let yourself go and start looking out for others. New Love starts when you stop caring about what you can get from this world and begin to seek things you can give it.

What Love Is

This love I'm talking about is much greater than the love we believe we show. This love is unexplainable, unreasonable, and outrageous. This love never ceases and will continue forever.

This love is the love of a father who sent his son to die for the whole world. This is what God did for us when He sent Jesus into this world. He lived a perfect life and then CHOSE to die for the sins we committed. All this just so we could be together with Him. We don't deserve this love. We did nothing for it and we receive it whether we want it or not. How much stronger can a love get? His love for us goes to the end of the Universe and back again. When it comes to love, God's Love surpasses all. God's Love is not like the love of this world. God's Love is much deeper and real. When love fails you God's Love will be there. This Love seems unreal, but in truth this Love can be shown in this world. We just have to realize what exactly this Love is.

A love like this can't be bought or even earned. Nothing you do or ever will do can make Love, love you anymore. Love loves you because it's Love. Love loves you when you're happy; Love loves you when you're sad. Even when you have failed to love, Love still loves you. There is nothing you can do to escape Love. Love will never fail, Love will never die. Love will see you to the end. It is Love that brought us here and it' is His love that we will rest in for eternity

This Love doesn't care what you say, or how you say it. Love only cares that you are there. Also Love cares! It cares for you through it all. With Love you don't have to worry about messing up. Love will love you no matter what. Love doesn't care what you look like or what you wear. Love doesn't look at where you came from or even where you are going. Love looks at you, and loves you just how you are! You don't have to change or get in shape for Love. Love doesn't want you to be anyone but yourself. Love takes you for exactly who you are and Love loves you for that.

Love gives you freedom to live, for you know you always have Love to run back to. With this freedom to live you now have the capacity to love and love freely. When you love, love with everything. Don't hold anything back. Let your love go! Love others to the extent that the real love, God's love, will shine through. Make your love count. I only hope and pray that we can find some way to show a small glimpse of this Love to the world before hate takes over and true love is forgotten.

1 Corinthians 13

"Though I speak with the tongues of men and of angles, but have not love, I have become sounds brass or a clanging cymbal. And though I have the gift of prophecy, and understand all mysteries and knowledge, and though I have all faith, so that I could remove mountains, but have not love, I am nothing. And though I bestow all my goods to feed the poor, and though I give my body to be burned, but have not love, it profits me nothing. Love suffers long and is kind; loves does not envy; loves does not parade itself, is not puffed up; does not behave rudely, does not seeks its own, is not provoked, thinks no evil; dos not rejoice in iniquity, but rejoices in truth; bears all things, believes all things, hopes all things, endures all things. Love never fails. But whether there are prophecies, they will fail; whether there are tongues, they will cease; whether there is knowledge, it will vanish away. For we know in part and we prophesy in part. But when that which is perfect has come, then that which is in part will be done away. When I was a child, I spoke as a child, u understood as a child, I thought as a child; but when I became a man, I put away childish things. For now we see in a mirror, dimly, but then face to face. Now I know in part, but then I shall know just as I also am known. And now abide faith, hope, love, these three; but the greatest of these is love."

It's a CHOICE

I'd like to say love is always easy, but sometimes it's not. Many times our love is tested. Love can hurt. Your friends might betray you, your wife may ignore you, your kids could disobey you; these all hurt us, but does that mean we should stop our love? Can we keep loving even after we are hurt? What is the extent of our love?

You have to choose to start loving someone and you choose to stop. Love is a choice! Nothing someone does can keep you from loving them. That's what makes love so beautiful, it's our choice! No one else makes the decision for us. It's all our own. So to come back to the question; "Should we stop our love?" well that's your decision. But I would hope you wouldn't choose the easy way out.

The easy thing to do is let hate take over. Hate fills our hearts with jealousy and pride. Hate hardens our hearts. Loving someone can be difficult. It takes effort. You have to fight and work at it. No one is perfect, and many times people will fail you. People have flaws, imperfections. We lie, cheat, steal. It's in our nature to inflict pain. But if we let these things stop our love we have lost. We can't let hate win. Yes; it will be difficult, but love must endure. How much more enjoyable is it to love? Love that endures is something you can build a life on. Love that lasts is something everyone is searching for.

Love doesn't have to say anything. More often than not love is shown through silence. Now this does not mean that love is quiet. Once we realize what love is we must show it! Anyone can say they love someone; that is easy. The real challenge comes with showing it. Showing love means showing up. To show love you must care. Care enough to listen and listen intently. Don't just talk to talk, talk to learn. Learn about someone, then show them you care. If love isn't moving then what is it? You can't set back on love. Love is action. So please, don't be afraid to move! And please, choose to love. Without love there is nothing. So above EVERYTHING else, LOVE!

"Owe no one anything except to love one another, for he who loves another has fulfilled the law." Romans 13:8

Talking to Love

The real love is God Himself. God is not just a symbol of love; He is Love. We would know nothing of love or even be able to understand what little we know about it if it were not for God. Not only did He show us outrageous love by creating us, but He showed us even more by coming to earth as human, living with us, and then dying for us. In His little time on earth Jesus showed us what love truly looked like. In His everyday life He taught us that love is shown through compassion and friendship. He helped us to see that love truly begins after you give up yourself; ultimately showing this as He died on the cross for our sins. This is why when it comes to love there is no one better to talk to than Love Himself.

"These words are not my own; only what God allowed me…"

12/05/2010

Dear Lord,

Please help me to not lose the LOVE! Love like, I have nothing else. Love people unconditionally. Love like there is no tomorrow. Help me to love people for who they are. Love them no matter what they do to me. And love them always. No matter how I feel or what I'm doing, help me to take the time to love. LOVE, no matter what anyone says, is a choice. You must choose to love someone. Love doesn't just happen, it's not a feeling. Yes, it is emotional, but the days when you feel nothing, you still must love. These days are when you must make that choice. You must choose to love that person, rain or shine, light or dark, good or bad. No matter what happens or what they do, love them and care for them. For this is how God loves us. He loves us unconditionally, without ceasing, never failing. This is the only definition of love I want to know. If I ever lose the capacity or capability of this LOVE, Lord take me. For if I don't love then I am not deserving of life. Love is all we have, and LOVE is all we need. You are the Love that gave Life it's name. Dear Lord, please help me to find You and Your Love.

Amen.

2/21/11

Dear Lord,

I have almost come to the conclusion that I will never have anyone but my Lord Jesus Christ. This is not a bad thing at all, but still it gets to me sometimes. I give my heart to everyone I see. If you need something I'll help you. If I have something you want, take it. I'll be there in a heartbeat if you need comfort, and I'm here to talk anytime you want. All these things go for everyone in the entire world. It doesn't matter who you are, I am totally at your disposal. And it is not because I think I am better than you. We are all sinners, and I have most likely sinned more than most. Without God in my life I am a wretched, perverted, twisted, son of a father who is just as bad. If I had my way I would be doing things that I wanted to do. I would seek things such as sex, wealth, and fame. These things can be very appealing. Thankfully, I have been changed, and not by my own strength, but by God's unchanging love for me. This is why I am who I am. Because I want nothing more for you than for you to be happy and joyous; without sadness. I need not to worry about my life for I want nothing of this world. God please help me to be content with You and You only! I want nothing more than You and Your love, please let me see you.

Amen.

4/01/11

Dear Lord,

I try to look past it, I try to drown it out. The daily battle of life takes over and I forget all about it. I think I'm here to achieve something. I start believing I was put here to build a reputation. My life at first seems full but then I realize deep down I'm really empty. Sometimes I feel like love isn't enough, that it might let me down. I'm telling myself one big lie. I must realize love is EVERYTHING! Without love I have no heart. If my heart is not there then I no longer live. To live is to love, THAT'S IT! It hurts too much to hate. It may seem easy at the time, but as life goes on you start wondering if there is more. Even though it seems hard, to love is easy! No one should have to do anything to receive your love, and there should be nothing they can do to make you stop giving love to them. Just Love; for if I don't love, Lord please kill me.

Amen.

4/15/11

Dear Lord,

I don't know what I'm doing, I don't know where I am, I don't know where I'm going. All I know is I'm here and I'm living. That alone is enough to glorify You. The only reason I am here is for you LORD. Nothing else on this earth satisfies me the way Your work does. I long to work! Put me where You want me; help me to go where You want me to go. I am a vessel for You, and that is all. The words I speak are not my own, the people I reach are not by my hand, and the Love I show is not my love. It is ALL You! Dear Lord, I go not for my own accomplishments, but only to further Your word. I want others to know of the peace and love I have found in You and in You only. I can't live without You. I don't want anyone else to either. Push me to go, take me to places I didn't think I could take myself. Help me to let myself go! Take my life and use it for Your will; for if I'm not doing Your work I don't want to live. Kill me Lord, and please help me to live for You. I want to let my life go!

Amen.

3

WHAT IF THERE WASN'T?

We cling so strongly to that promise of eternal life, and with good right! God clearly states that promise to us in John 3:16. If you believe in Him (Jesus Christ) you will have everlasting life. If this was the only verse you ever read from the Bible, and you believed it whole heartedly, it would be enough. And you would be given the amazing and unbelievable gift of eternal life, getting to live one with God forever. If this was the only promise you ever heard it would be more than enough. This promise shows the full extent of God's love for you. But realistically, this is only one of the so many promises God has in store for us. The deeper you dive into His word the more He will reveal to you.

Of course there is a Heaven. That is not what I'm arguing. But if there wasn't would there still be a reason to worship and glorify God? Without that promise is it possible for us as "Believers" to still live out life to honor God? Could we still do it?

"For God so loved the world that He gave is only begotten Son, that whosoever believes in Him should not perish but have everlasting life." John 3:16

Have you ever read any further than John 3:16? If not that is perfectly okay, but I will admit you'd be missing out. If you ever got far enough you would find that God has something else He would like you to know. In reading John 10 you see that Jesus is talking to the people as a "Shepherd." He tells them "I am the door of the sheep", and that through Him is the ONLY way to heaven. Reading a little further Jesus also reveals one of the main reasons why He came. In John 10:10 Jesus tells us that He came they we may have life and have it more abundantly! Do we truly understand this? God doesn't just want us to live life, but to truly LIVE life! He doesn't want us just sitting back on His promises, but living them out. Yes, of course there is more to life than this world, for this world is only the beginning. But why is it that once we are saved we sometimes begin to live life like this world doesn't matter?

"The thief does not come except to steal, and to kill, and to destroy. I have come that they may have life, and that they may have it more abundantly." John 10:10

I believe we are too caught up in ourselves to see the real picture. We were created! By no power of our own were we put here. There was nothing whatsoever that we did to gain life. It was all God! Do we realize that it is a blessing to live? We started as nothing and He MADE us who we are. If he wants us to die we, we die. If He allows us to live, we live. He can do whatever He wants; He is God! But isn't it awesome that He makes us promises and always keeps them?! Unlike us He sticks to His word strongly. Anything He says He does.

God loves us so deeply that He created us. He showed us that love through sending His son Jesus Christ. And in letting us live in this world He created in such detail, He made it evident that His love is REAL! So after knowing all these promises, what would be enough for us? If were given nothing else but our time on this earth, would that be enough?

"Know that the LORD, He is God; it is He who has made us, and not we ourselves; we are His people and the sheep of the pasture." Psalm 100:3

Truthfully this question is scary. To think about it means that we must recommend that this life is it. After we die we go back to whence we came; nothing. And if we start as nothing and end as nothing, then what does that make us right now? Your immediate reaction might be nothing, but that would be until you start looking at yourself. You are so much more than nothing! There is so much detail and precision about your body and mind that to say you are nothing is an understatement.

Think of life; and everything in it. The good, the bad, the worst; God wants you to enjoy it all! Yes; life seems hard at times, but that's the beauty of it! Making mistakes and going through hard times is part of life. Life is about learning. God made life so intricate that no one could ever come even close to learning everything in one lifetime. One could study a specific species of plant their whole life, and think they know everything about it. Then the day before they die that plant could do something that totally surprised them. That is for a reason! God wants you to explore life and find His glory in it! For He is in everything!

"Let the heavens rejoice, and let the earth be glad; let the sea roar, and all its fullness; let the field be joyful, and all that is in it. The all the trees of the woods will rejoice before the Lord." Psalm 96:11-12

Each and every day in this world is filled with wonder and amazement. The things we get to do, feel, smell and touch. If you think about it life is truly astonishing. If nothing else the ability to eat and taste alone is worthy of God's praise. I don't know about you but I love to eat, probably too much. There are so many different foods on this earth that I could never try them all. The ability to taste sweetness and bitterness, to feel hot and cold, to touch rough and smooth. God made all this possible! What more could we ask for? We have been given a life that we could never dream up. Every single aspect of life God has drawn out in ultimate detail. Not one thing on this earth went unnoticed or forgotten. There aren't any loopholes, everything is there. He made this world for us, and He wants us to live in it. God wants you to enjoy life, and everything in it. These things didn't just happen by accident. God put everything on earth for a distinct purpose and a specific role. Just being able to be part of this magnificent creation is a blessing we can't understand.

"He does great things past finding out, Yes, wonders without numbers. – How then can I answer Him, and choose my words to reason with Him?" Job 9:10, 14

Most things of this world we can't understand. And truthfully, we probably never will. Who are we to try and figure out God? If God is intelligent enough to make the brain that was put in the man that thought up *Differential Equations* (my downfall), then there is no way I could ever come close to figuring Him out. The ability to breath even fathoms me. We try to become so self-sufficient, yet every few seconds we have to breathe. How naïve are we? Man constantly wants more and more knowledge. If we could we would be our own God. But that is something we couldn't even comprehend. We have a hard enough time with eternity. Eternity to us cannot be comprehended. It is crazy even to think about. Many people have tried to put a definition on it, but none have gained knowledge of its entirety. Thankfully, we don't have to know all things to live.

Don't be scared you don't know everything. You're not supposed to! Don't let life overwhelm you. Enjoy life. Constantly striving for knowledge is no that answer. For what is knowledge but what God makes it? Don't let knowledge be your only goal in life. If you are really looking to strive for something strive for "LOVE". Love is what God has ultimately shown us. Strive to love and love without ceasing. Without love what is life anyways? It's definitely not the life I know. That is one more reason to thank God for the life He made for us.

So if there wasn't a heaven would you live your life any different? This is a hard question even to ask myself. I don't like thinking about it, it truly scares me. To think that this world is it and after I die I'm done is heartbreaking. But still the question is, if there wasn't a heaven would there still be reason to worship God?

So.........Is God enough?

What if we were only given creation? Could we find the meaning of life if all we were given was this life? Even with the promise of eternity, finding the meaning of life is difficult. We believe we can find things in this world to satisfy our every need, but that's just our foolish pride. Pride is our number one enemy. This is because prides is essentially ourselves battling ourselves. And in this battle you always win. Unfortunately in that battle of finding the meaning of life winning is not the best option. In this life you find more meaning in losing yourself.

"Whoever seeks to save his life will lose it, and whoever loses his life will preserve it." Luke 17:33

I've seen many times that the key to life is coming the very end of it, then praising Christ. When you are at the end of life you have nothing. When you have nothing you forget about what you have and realize what you have been given. At this point you forget yourself and look to the only one that means anything, God. Once you start looking to God you have done it; you just found the meaning of life.

Whether we like it or not we were made for one purpose; to glorify God. In order to glorify God you must seek Him in your daily life. Living in this world day to day is what it all comes down to. One day we could be here; the next we could be gone. We are not promised anything. It is all a gift. So what are we doing with our gift? Are we making the most of the days that we are granted? Or; more to the point, are we seeing the work of God in our day to day life?

Many believe God only shows up in life on rare occasions. I would have to drastically beg to differ. God is constantly at work in our lives every second of everyday. God is everywhere. All we have to do is look and listen. Often times we get the look part down, but we forget to listen. We wonder why we don't see anything when half the time we are looking in the wrong direction.

"Then He said to them, "Take heed what you hear. With the same measure you use, it will be measured to you; and to you who hear, more will be given." Mark 4:24

Listening to God is sometimes difficult. At times we let this world or ourselves drown God out. Pride is once again the leading factor for our incoherence. We get too comfortable in our lives and think we don't need God. We sit back and try to tell ourselves we did this on our own. When pride sets in we no longer think of this life as a gift, but instead think of it as something we deserve. We try to plan out our future. Focus so much on what is coming next that we forget the present. Yes; planning for the future is great, but don't dwell on it! Don't worry about tomorrow, for who knows if it will even come! Slow down and take each day as it is granted to you. Live life like a gift, because that's exactly what it is!

"Therefore do not worry about tomorrow, for tomorrow will worry about its own things. Sufficient for the day is its own trouble." Matthew 6:34

You must trust TOTALLY in the LORD! I'll admit that trusting is tough. In order to trust you must be vulnerable. Being vulnerable is not easy or comfortable. No one wants to be vulnerable. We all want that sense of security; that backup plan. Leaping headfirst into the darkness is not our style. We like to know exactly what we are getting into before we do it. Risks, rewards, drawbacks, everything; we want to know it all beforehand. But guess what, we don't get to. There are things we will never understand and concepts we can't ever comprehend. We just have to face it. We are not in control and there is nothing we can do about it. Our days are numbered on this earth. It is inevitable, we WILL die one day. Although we cannot see it, we know that day is coming. We can try to run from it, but we will never get away. Death is something none of us can truly understand, that is because we are still living! So why then do we fear death? Stop worrying about things you know nothing about! Stop worrying about what the future holds and start living in the life you have been granted now!

"Trust in the Lord with all your heart, and lean not on your own understanding; in all your ways acknowledge Him, and He shall direct your paths." Proverbs 3:5-6

Trust in God to show you the reason for living today and praise Him continuously for giving it to you. Don't forget to live in the day you are given and trust in God to do what He wants with your future. God gave you this life for you to live, so live! Draw closer to God daily and ask Him to reveal His truths. For our main purpose in life is not to know ourselves but to better know God. So seek Him, listen, and let yourself be open and vulnerable to the truths He wants to reveal to us.

Psalm 104:19-34

"He appointed the moon for seasons; the sun knows it's going down.
You make darkness, and it is night, in which
all the beasts of the forest creep about.
The young lions roar after their prey, and seek their food from God.
When the sun rises, they gather together and lie down in their dens.
Man goes out to his work and to his labor until the evening.
O LORD, how manifold are Your works! In wisdom You
have made them all. The earth if full of Your possessions
This great and wide sea, in which are innumerable
teeming things, living things both small and great.
There the ships sail about; there is that Leviathan
which you have made to play there.
These all wait for You, that you may give
them their food in due season.
What you give them they gather in; You open
Your hand, they are filled with good.
You hide Your face, they are troubled; You take away
their breath, they die and return to their dust.
You send forth Your Spirit, they are created;
and You renew the face of the earth.
May the glory of the LORD endure forever;
May the LORD rejoice in His works.
He looks on the earth, and it trembles; He
touches the hills, and they smoke.
I will sing to the LORD as long as I live; I will
sing praise to my God while I have my being.
May my meditation be sweet to Him; I will be glad in the LORD."

4

WHY DOES IT HAVE TO STOP?

Why does it have to stop? Why does that sense of purpose and fulfillment have to leave when we go through those doors? What is it about that place? Is it any different than my home, my car, the school I go to, or even Wal-Mart? I feel like I have two different mind sets. One that is totally focused on the main purpose of life, and another that is focused on me, and what I want. I have one that is excited for what the day brings, and another that is fearful of what might happen. I have one that loves, and one that hates. I have one that is patient and one that can't stand to wait. No matter what I do it feels like they are always at war with each other. Neither one wins, it's just a constant battle. Will I ever be one person?

If it wasn't clear already the doors I'm speaking of are the doors of the church. Also, the two different mind sets are my own selfish mind set, and the mind of God the Holy Spirit gives me. When in church it's easy. Everyone has the same thing in mind, worship

God. Usually nothing else distracts you and you can focus totally on what God is speaking to you. This seems awesome! God reveals things in your life that you need to change, and in your mind there is nothing that will stop you from changing them. While in church you feel invincible, powerful, and purposeful. You think of ways to reach the lost. You think of ideas to help the community and give back to the poor. You intend on giving more and receiving less. You realize one really doesn't need all these possessions. God shows you that most things of this life really don't matter, and that the only thing that will truly last in eternity is LOVE. All this seems so easy to comprehend when inside those doors. When you leave you feel motivated and confident of what the LORD will use you for. But then reality of the world strikes, and once outside those doors something changes.

Once you take one step outside those doors you are hit with what the world has to offer. For example, one usually goes out to eat on a Sunday; it's just what people do. The topic of the table is hardly ever about what was just spoken in church, but most often what the new weeks is going to bring. We are always looking ahead. After eating lunch we usually go back home, lay around the house, watch television. I can't think of one time that I ever reflected on what God had spoken to me about in church. I just told myself I will do it later, or I had thought about that enough at church. But wasn't it just at church that I told myself I would have a purpose? Dinner comes around and you eat and maybe talk about what shows are on tonight, or how much gas is going to be tomorrow. Another chance to reflect that none of us take advantage of. Before you know it you have fallen asleep, and you wake up the next morning and head off to school or work. By this time you have forgotten almost everything that you said you would remember while at church. The world has won again.

This is all too common for every one of us. In no way am I saying that any of those things done on Sunday are bad or sinful. It is perfectly okay to relax and enjoy the things of this world. Where we go wrong is with our mind set, and why we do those things. Like I said, this mind set almost immediately changes when we leave through those doors of the church. When we leave we start thinking of ourselves, most of the time we think, "I'm hungry." So at this time food is all we can think about. Don't get me wrong, food is fantastic. I love food! But why are we eating? Are we eating to keep ourselves alive or because we want to be sustained so we can live longer for the glory of God? Kind of drastic comparison, but it makes you think. Why do we do things? Do we relax because we are tired, or so we can be well rested to work hard in the week to come? When talking about each other's week what are we doing that for? I would like to say it's so I can remember people's schedules and learn more about their lives. But quite honestly, I'll forget what someone told me not minutes after they said it. So if that's not my purpose, then what is my purpose? Where did that motivation I had not an hour earlier go to? Is it still there? I believe it is.

Why does it have to stop? This motivation and purpose we had in church doesn't have to stop at the door, it can go with us. If we let it, it can go anywhere we go, because this motivation and purpose we speak of is in fact God Himself. The Holy Spirit is what you felt in church, and what gave you all those ideas for the lost and the poor. The Holy Spirit is the one that humbled you, and made you think less of yourself and more about what you can do for others. The Holy Spirit did all this. And do you want to know another secret?........ The Holy Spirit is NOT confined to the walls of the church. As a matter of fact this universe can't confine the Holy Spirit, because the Holy Spirit is the presence of God and God is everywhere and in everything. He is omnipresent and omnipotent. He was here before, He is here now, and He will be here forever to come.

"And I will pray the Father and He will give you another Helper, that He may abide with you forever, even the Spirit of truth, whom the world cannot receive because it neither sees Him nor knows Him; but you know Him for He dwells with you and will be in you." John 14:16

So why do we think He stops at the doorstep of the church? Those same feelings and thoughts you acquire while at church can be felt outside just as well. It's not some mysterious or mystical magic. It's not ritualistic or even the power of a fellowship of Believers. It is entirely God! The problem is once outside the doors we get caught up in the world and think more of ourselves than what ourselves can do for God. Think about when you go to church. You go for a purpose, to praise and worship God, and to hear His word preached. Having a purpose helps you focus entirely on God, not yourself. When all the focus is on God you tend to hear what He is saying to you. Whether through song, preaching, or your mind; God speaks to you. The problem is that God is always speaking to us, even outside of church. The fact is half the time we don't want to listen.

Why does that purpose stop at the door? Can't that purpose carry on into our lives? What would happen if we lived life with a purpose? A purpose to entirely and willfully glorify God. This would be a life where you are constantly seeking what God wants you to do. Every decision is based on His will and not your own. You think about others before yourself. If you have to deny yourself to bring someone else up, then do it! Living life for your own purpose doesn't really have any purpose at all. In real time, how long does your life last? This world is not the end; not even close. Never start living for your own name. Your name doesn't matter! Most likely in a hundred years, no one on earth is going to even remember you. The only name that matters is God's name. That is the name you should be living for. Living for God's name gives you purpose, and without purpose we get lost in life.

Getting lost in life is easy, everyone does it. We feel obligated to participate and socialize. Work takes up most of our time, and anytime left is spent working on things we deem important, such as working out, reading, or watching television. These things on their own are not sinful, and I'm not saying you must quit doing them. By all means keep enjoying the things of life! But what I'm saying is don't just do them to be doing them, do them for a purpose! Participate and socialize with the intent to get to know more people. And don't just know people, but learn about them. Find out what makes them tick, and love them. Work with a mindset that you are trying to impress, even when no one is looking. Don't work for yourself, or your boss, or for anyone else on this earth; work at whatever job is given to you as if working for the LORD. (Colossians 3:23) And in your free time, by all means work out, read, and watch television. You can do all these things with a purpose to Glorify God; you just have to find that purpose and pursue it.

"He who observes the day, observes it to the Lord; and he who does not observe the day, to the Lord he does not observe it. He who eats, eats to the Lord, for he gives God thanks; and he who does not eat, to the Lord he does not eat, and gives God thanks. For none of us lives to himself, and no one dies to himself." Romans 14:6-7

Without a purpose you start doing things for yourself. It is all too simple to start working on yourself for your own benefit. I fall into this trap all too often. The main reason deep down of why I work out is to honor God. I work out to better my body to pursue the works God has in store for me. I also want people to see that I work out; not so they will see me; but so they will see God through the fact that I work as hard as I possibly can. This is what I deep down work out for, but far too often this is not the case. I start working out to better myself. I look at myself and think I look good. Then I think; "I did this", and that confidence turns to arrogance and pride ever so easily. Sometimes it's the opposite. I look at myself and think I don't look good enough. So then I work out even harder........but what for? At that point what am I working for? At this point I'm living for my own name, plain and simple. The very thing I didn't want to do. Almost every aspect of life is like this. As long as you are pursuing God in what you do, and doing it with a heart set on Him; there is no shame in what you do. This could be anything from watching television, playing basketball, fishing, hunting, sewing, playing video games, relaxing, sleeping, eating ...... the list goes on and on. Anything you can think of you can do for God. The bad thing is it goes both ways. Anything you do can also be done for yourself. This is the number one reason why God stops at the doors. Once we get into the world we forget about that purpose we have in God and start seeing what we can do for ourselves.

Never lose that focus, always have a purpose. God is with you always and will direct you down the path He has for you. All you have to do is stop and listen. Our lives are busy and getting busier every day, but we must slow down and listen. Combat pride with humility, and let the Holy Spirit direct your life. Think little of yourself and much more of others. Never start living for your own name; instead live to glorify the only name that matters, God's name. Live to lift up His name and His name only. Live life with a purpose and remember that IT doesn't have to stop at the doors.

5
PRIDE

I have made attempts to write this chapter over pride multiple times. Each instance being even worse than the attempt before. I felt that this portion over pride had to be perfect. I wanted it to be something that would change lives. In it I would talk about how pride sets in when we don't even think about it. How pride can't stand up against forgiveness. And even in our weakness we can be prideful. I had all these lists and points I wanted to get across. I thought I had pride all figured out. I just knew that what I would write would help people. And that's when it hit me.....This was ALL ABOUT ME. At some point I stopped writing about fighting "Pride" and started writing something that pointed back to myself. For this I say I am sorry. Pride got me. My fault came when I made it too complicated. Life is messy, and so is our battle with pride. There is no definite remedy. I thought I knew everything there was to know about pride, but in the end I only confused myself even further. That is why this will be a short message. I feel like I know less now about pride than when I started. The more I delved deeper into what pride was the more I realized how big the battle is. But one thing I did find is the weapon I will choose to fight pride with. This weapon is not meekness, humility, or a kind heart. It is something far more **influential.** The weapon I choose to fight my battle with pride will be the example of "sacrifice" Jesus Christ showed me on the cross, and the new definition he gave to it:

Sacrifice:
Choosing others over yourself no matter what the cost or circumstances; not giving into the fear of not knowing who you will become in the process

With this example and new definition I can go out and fight the battle against pride, myself, and life. In everything that comes about holding true to the promise that I know exactly who I am and who I will become. And that will forever and always be a child of God.

"For He made Him who knew no sin *to be* sin for us, that we might become the righteousness of God in Him." 2 Corinthians 5:21

My Prayer....

My only hope from this book is to help point toward the One who showed us how to live life. This collection started out of my prayers to Him. At time when I doubted, times when I was filled with guilt, and when I thought I had no love left to give; He showed me differently.

I pray you cling to what He shows you. Don't be afraid to let go of who you have become and allow Him to make you new. Each day rediscovering the definition of life in Christ.

Your Prayer....

Each person has a different story. That's what makes life so awesome! There is only one Christ, but He makes Himself evident through so many ways they can never be numbered. Saying this I would love to hear your story and how God is showing himself through the life you live. Not only to rejoice with you and pray for you, but also for encouragement. For the longest time I thought I had to do it on my own. One of the many prideful things God corrected through humility. I didn't want to ask for help, but God gave us the Church and each other for a reason.

If you would like to send your prayer to me you can do so by going to http://differentdefinition.azurewebsites.net/

and clicking MyStory or by sending it by mail to:

1825 E Republic Rd Apt 203
Springfield, MO 65804

Hope to hear from you! ☺

References

The Holy Bible, New King James Version. Nashville: Thomas Nelson Publishers, 1983. Print

"sin" [def 1] *Merriam-Webster.com.* Merriam-Webster, 2013.Web. 14 June 2013.

"love" [def 1] *Merriam-Webster.com.* Merriam-Webster, 2013. Web. 1 December 2013.

"sin." [def 1] *Noah Webster's 1828 American Dictionary of the English Language.* 2014. http://1828.mshaffer.com/d/word/sin (24 March 2014).

CPSIA information can be obtained at www.ICGtesting.com
Printed in the USA
LVOW08s0026170614

390291LV00001B/3/P